Ryan Murphy

Children, go where I send thee

Bass and drums

Children, go where I send thee

African-American Spiritual
arr. **RYAN MURPHY**

cresc. poco a poco

Children, go where I send thee

African-American Spiritual
arr. RYAN MURPHY

OXFORD UNIVERSITY PRESS, MUSIC DEPARTMENT, GREAT CLARENDON STREET, OXFORD OX2 6DP
The Moral Rights of the Arranger have been asserted. Photocopying this copyright material is ILLEGAL.

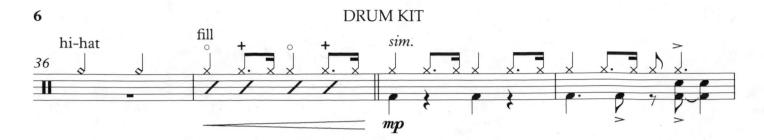

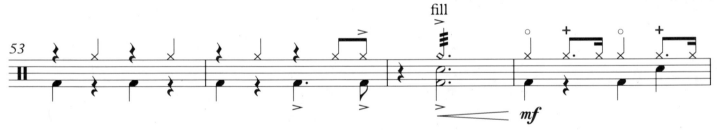

X831 Children, go where I send thee MURPHY

ISBN 978-0-19-355853-3

9 780193 558533